CLASSIC CAKES

CLASSIC
Australian
CAKES

From Lamingtons to Swiss Roll
ALICE MAY

ALLEN & UNWIN

First published in 1993 by
Allen & Unwin
9 Atchison Street
St Leonards NSW 2065
Australia

Created and produced by
Modern Times Pty Ltd
P.O. Box 908
Bondi Junction NSW 2022,
Australia

© Modern Times Pty Ltd

National Library of Australia
Cataloguing-in-Publication entry:

May, Alice L.
        Classic Australian cakes.

        Includes index.
        ISBN 1 86373 545 3.

        1. Cake - Australia. 2. Cookery, Australian. I. Title.

641.86530994

Produced by Mandarin Offset, Hong Kong

CONTENTS

INTRODUCTION

CLASSIC CAKES is a tribute to the great home-cooking of our mothers and grandmothers. The kitchen was once the only place to be. There was always the smell of freshly baked cakes in the air. Here you could help to beat the sweet and sticky cake mixtures and await your turn to scrap the discarded bowl with your fingertips. Then the hot, sweet-smelling cakes would emerge from the oven and be left to cool on wire racks awaiting a generous coating of icing. Everyday was cake day and school lunches always included a treat. Christmas time brought about a flurry of baking with big bowls of fruit soaking in the rarely opened sherry. There was always a little something in the cupboard in case friends dropped by or just to have with a nice cup of tea. The cooking was honest, sincere and simple.

This book reminds us of home, heart and hearth and of gentler times when life was less chaotic.

Apple Slice Favourite

4 medium-sized green cooking apples
4 tablespoons water
4 tablespoons sugar
A little fresh lemon rind or 3 or 4 cloves

Pastry
185 g (6 ½ oz) plain (all-purpose) flour
½ level teaspoon baking powder
pinch of salt
75 g (3 oz) butter
2 slightly rounded tablespoons sugar
1 egg, lightly beaten
½ teaspoon vanilla

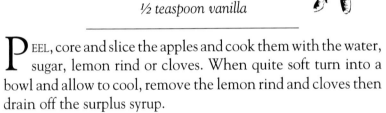

Peel, core and slice the apples and cook them with the water, sugar, lemon rind or cloves. When quite soft turn into a bowl and allow to cool, remove the lemon rind and cloves then drain off the surplus syrup.

Preheat oven to 180 deg C (350 deg F). Lightly grease with butter an 18 cm (7 in) springform pan (or sandwich pan). Sift the flour, baking powder and salt. Beat the butter and sugar until creamy, light and fluffy. Add the egg and vanilla beating very well. Mix in the sifted flour making a firm dough. Knead only until the outside is smooth. Using slightly more than half the dough, roll it out to fit into the pan, covering the sides too. Add the apple and then cover with the remainder of the pastry rolled to fit the top. Pinch a frill around the edges, make three or four vents in the pastry to allow the steam to escape then paint with beaten egg white. Bake for 50 to 60 minutes.

9

BANANA BREAD

---

250 g (9 oz) plain (all-purpose) flour
2 teaspoons baking powder
½ teaspoon salt
50 g (2 oz) butter
125 g (4 ½ oz) caster (superfine) sugar
2 large or 3 small bananas
1 egg
25 g (1 oz) walnuts, roughly chopped
3 tablespoons yoghurt

PREHEAT oven to 180 deg C (350 deg F). Lightly grease with butter a 18 cm x 9 cm x 9 cm (7 in x 3 ½ x 3 ½ in) loaf pan and line base with baking parchment. Sift the flour with the baking powder and salt.

Beat the butter and sugar until creamy, light and fluffy. Mash the bananas and mix with the egg. Add the egg and bananas gradually to the creamed mixture beating all the time. Mix in the walnuts. Gently fold in by hand the sifted flour alternately with the yoghurt. Pour the mixture into the prepared pan and bake for 1 hour or until the cake has shrunk slightly away from the sides of the pan. Turn out onto wire rack to cool.

Mix cakes lightly but thoroughly. Too much mixing makes cakes heavy. Insufficient mixing results in sodden patches and a coarse uneven texture.

BASIC SPONGE

125 g (4 ½ oz) plain (all-purpose) flour
1 teaspoon baking powder
pinch of salt
3 eggs, separated
160 g (5 ½ oz) caster (superfine) sugar
1 teaspoon butter, melted
3 tablespoons hot water

PREHEAT oven to 180 deg C (350 deg F). Grease two 18 cm (7 in) springform pans (or sandwich pans) lightly with butter and line with baking parchment. Sift the flour with the baking powder and salt.

Beat the egg whites until they form soft peaks; gradually add the sugar until the mixture is thick. Add the egg yolks all at the one time, beating until they are completely combined. Sift the flour over the egg mixture. Fold in the melted butter and hot water. Pour the mixture into the prepared pans and bake for 20 minutes or until the top of the cake springs back when lightly touched and the cakes have shrunk slightly away from the sides of the trays. Cool in the pans for 5 minutes before turning out onto wire racks to cool. Sandwich together with jam and whipped cream. Decorate the top of the cake with glacé icing.

For the best results, chill cream well before whipping and whip in a chilled bowl.

BOILED CRUSHED PINEAPPLE CAKE

325 g (11 ½ oz) plain (all-purpose) flour
2 level teaspoons baking powder
¼ teaspoon bicarbonate of soda (baking soda)
150 g (5 oz) butter
225 g (8 oz) sugar
1 x 425 g (15 oz) can crushed pineapple
450 g (1 lb) mixed fruit (currants, sultanas (golden raisins), raisins)
2 eggs, beaten
¼ teaspoon mixed spice
1 small dessertspoon apple cider vinegar

PREHEAT oven to 180 deg C (350 deg F). Generously grease a 23 cm (9 in) springform pan with butter and line with baking parchment. Sift the flour, bicarbonate of soda and baking powder together.

Combine the butter, sugar, pineapple, and mixed fruit in a saucepan. Bring to the boil, stirring well, then simmer for 3 minutes. Cool.

Beat the eggs until light and lemon coloured and add them gradually to the cooled mixture. Add the sifted flour, mixed spice and vinegar, mixing well. Pour into the prepared pan and bake for between 1 and 2 hours or until the cake has shrunk slightly away from the sides of the pan.

BOILED FRUIT CAKE

310 g (11 oz) plain (all-purpose) flour
1 teaspoon baking powder
100 g (4 oz) butter
250 g (9 oz) sugar
250 ml (8 fl oz) cold water
100 g (4 oz) currants
350 g (12 oz) sultanas (golden raisins)
50 g (2 oz) mixed peel
1 teaspoon nutmeg
1 teaspoon mixed spice
1 tablespoon lemon juice
2 eggs
2 teaspoons golden (light corn) syrup
1/2 teaspoon bicarbonate of soda (baking soda)
1 tablespoon boiling water

13

Preheat oven to 160 deg C (325 deg F). Generously grease a 23 cm (9 in) springform pan with butter and line with baking parchment. Sift the flour together with the baking powder.

Combine the butter, sugar, cold water, fruit, spices and lemon juice in a saucepan. Bring to the boil, stirring well, then boil for 3 minutes. Cool.

Beat the eggs until light and lemon coloured and add them gradually to the cooled mixture. Add the sifted flour and then the golden syrup. Lastly add the bicarbonate of soda which has been dissolved in the boiling water. Pour into the prepared tin and bake for about 2 hours or until the cake has shrunk slightly away from the sides of the pan.

This cake improves with keeping. Wrap and store in an airtight container for at least three days before cutting.

To test if cakes are cooked:
Small Cakes — The cake is elastic when pressed lightly
with finger tips. Sponge Cakes — The cake shrinks from
the tin, and is also elastic. Large Cakes — A skewer,
after being run through the centre of cake should come
out clean and dry.

BUTTERFLY CAKES

---

250 g (9 oz) plain (all-purpose) flour
2 teaspoons baking powder
pinch of salt
125 g (4 ½ oz) butter
185 g (6 ½ oz) sugar
2 large eggs, beaten
1 teaspoon vanilla
185 ml (6 ½ fl oz) milk
whipped cream
icing sugar

PREHEAT oven to 200 deg C (400 deg F). Grease patty pans (cup cake pans) lightly with butter or use paper cases. Sift the flour with the baking powder and salt.

Beat the butter and sugar until creamy, light and fluffy. Add the eggs one at a time, beating very well after each one is added. Mix in the vanilla. Gently fold in by hand the sifted flour alternately with the milk. Spoon the mixture into the prepared pans or paper cases until three-quarters full. Bake for 15 to 20 minutes or until the cakes are golden brown. Turn out onto wire racks to cool.

When cool cut a circle from the top of each cake. Fill with a spoonful of sweetened whipped cream. Cut the circle in half

16

and place on top of the cream to resemble butterfly wings. Dust with icing sugar.

CHERRY CAKE

225g (8 oz) plain (all-purpose) flour
½ teaspoon baking powder
¼ teaspoon salt
175 g (6 oz) butter or margarine
175 g (6 oz) sugar
2 eggs
milk
vanilla
75 g (3 oz) glacé cherries, halved
caster (superfine) sugar

P REHEAT oven to 180 deg C (350 deg F). Lightly grease with butter a 23 cm (9 in) springform pan or cake pan and line the base with baking parchment. Sift the flour with the baking powder and salt.

Beat the butter and sugar until creamy, light and fluffy. Add the eggs one at a time, beating very well after each one is added. Gently fold in by hand the sifted flour alternately with a little milk and the vanilla. Fold in most of the cherries reserving a few for the top. Pour into the prepared pan and place the reserved cherries on top and then sprinkle with caster sugar, to give a crisp, sugary surface. Bake for 1 hour or until the cake has shrunk slightly away from the sides of the pan.

CHOCOLATE ECLAIRS

fresh cream or Confectioners' custard
choux (cream puff) pastry
chocolate glacé icing

Choux (cream puff) pastry
60 g (2 ½ oz) plain (all-purpose) flour
175 ml (6 fl oz) water
60 g (2 ½ oz) butter
pinch of salt
2 eggs

PREHEAT oven to 200 deg C (400 deg F). Grease a baking tray (sheet) lightly with butter. Sift the flour.

Place the water and butter in a saucepan and bring to the boil over medium heat. Remove from heat and add the flour and salt to the mixture beating all the time. Cook over a low heat until the mixture forms a ball, stirring all the time. Cool slightly and add the eggs a little at a time until the mixture is smooth, soft and shiny.

Use a piping (pastry) bag fitted with a plain 1 cm or 1 ½ cm (½ in or ¾ in) nozzle to pipe fingers of paste about 9 to 10 cm (3 ½ in to 4 in) long onto the prepared tray. Keep the éclairs very even in size. Bake for about 30 to 40 minutes until the éclairs are well risen, golden-brown, and very light in texture.

Remove from oven and allow to cool slightly, slit down one side to allow the steam to escape, and put on a rack to cool. When they are quite cold, fill them with whipped cream or Confectioners' custard, and coat the top of each with chocolate glacé icing.

19

GROWING UP
ON THE
COCOA HABIT

CADBURYS

BOURNVILLE COCOA

The happy family habit

CREAM PUFFS

Drop spoonsful of choux (cream puff) pastry onto the baking tray (sheet) and cook for 20 minutes. When they are cold cut them open and fill them with whipped cream. A little glacé icing can be used to decorate them.

CHOCOLATE SPONGE

250 g (9 oz) plain (all-purpose) flour
2 teaspoons baking powder
1 teaspoon cream of tartar
½ teaspoon bicarbonate of soda (baking soda)
pinch of salt
100 g (4 oz) butter
375 g (13 oz) sugar
3 eggs
1 teaspoon vanilla
125 ml (4 ½ fl oz) milk
100 g (4 oz) dark cocoa powder dissolved in
125 ml (4 fl oz) hot water.

PREHEAT oven to 200 deg C (400 deg F). Grease three 18 cm (7 in) springform pans (or sandwich pans) lightly with butter and line bases with baking parchment. Sift the flour with the baking powder, cream of tartar, bicarbonate of soda and salt.

Beat the butter and sugar until creamy, light and fluffy. Add the eggs one at a time, beating very well after each one is added. Mix in by hand the sifted flour. Add the vanilla and fold in the milk and cocoa mixture. Pour the mixture into the prepared pans and bake for 15 to 20 minutes or until the cakes have shrunk slightly away from the sides of the pan. Turn the cakes out onto a wire rack to cool.

Open oven door as little as possible; do not slam it, as cold air entering oven may make the cake sink.

TRADITIONAL CHRISTMAS CAKE

185 g (6 ½ oz) glacé cherries, cut into halves
125 g (4 ½ oz) mixed peel
125 g (4 ½ oz) glacé apricots, diced small
125 g (4 ½ oz) figs, chopped
375 g (13 oz) raisins, cut into halves
185 g (6 ½ oz) currants
500 g (1 lb 1 oz) sultanas (golden raisins)
grated rind of 1 orange
grated rind of 1 lemon
4 tablespoons whisky or brandy
2 tablespoons plain (all-purpose) flour

250 g (9 oz) plain (all-purpose) flour
1 teaspoon cinnamon
½ teaspoon mixed spice
½ teaspoon grated nutmeg
250 g (9 oz) butter
250 g (9 oz) soft brown sugar
1 tablespoon treacle (molasses)
5 large eggs
An additional
three tablespoons whisky or brandy

M IX together the cherries, mixed peel, apricots, figs, raisins, currants and sultanas in a bowl with the orange and lemon rind. Add the whisky or brandy and cover the bowl. Leave to marinate for a minimum of 2 hours but preferably 24 hours. Just before using, sift 2 tablespoons of flour over the fruit and mix the flour through the fruit with your hands.

Preheat oven to 180 deg C (350 deg F). Generously grease a 28 cm (11 in) springform pan or cake pan with butter and line with two layers of brown paper and two layers of baking parchment. Sift the flour with the cinnamon, mixed spice and nutmeg.

Beat the butter and sugar until creamy, light and fluffy. Add the treacle (molasses) and then three eggs one at a time, beating very well after each one is added. Add a couple of tablespoons of the sifted flour to the creamed mixture to prevent it curdling then add the last two eggs and beat well. Fold in the flour and then the whisky or brandy. Lastly stir in the fruit. Mix well. Spoon the mixture carefully into the prepared pan and smooth the surface. Bake for five minutes at 180 deg C (350 deg F), then reduce the oven to 150 deg C (300 deg F). Cook for a further 3 hours or until a skewer comes out of the cake quite clean. It may even take a little longer than this. Cool in the tin.

A gradually decreasing heat is best for all cakes.

CINNAMON CAKE

225 g (8 oz) plain (all-purpose) flour
2 level teaspoons baking powder
2 teaspoons cinnamon
1 small teaspoon mixed spice
pinch of salt
100 g (4 oz) butter
175 g (6 oz) sugar
2 eggs
125 ml (4 1/2 fl oz) milk

PREHEAT oven to 180 deg C (350 deg F). Lightly grease with butter a 23 cm (9 in) springform pan or cake pan and line base with baking parchment. Sift the flour with the baking powder, cinnamon, mixed spice and salt.

Beat the butter and sugar until creamy, light and fluffy. Add the eggs one at a time, beating very well after each one is added. Mix in by hand the sifted flour and fold in the milk. Pour the mixture into the prepared pan and bake for 30 to 35 minutes or until the cake has shrunk slightly away from the sides of the pan. Turn the cake out onto a wire rack to cool.

COCONUT CAKE

185 g (6 ½ oz) plain (all-purpose) flour
2 teaspoons baking powder
2 large tablespoons butter
250 g (9 oz) sugar
2 eggs
2 tablespoons milk
3 tablespoons coconut

PREHEAT oven to 190 deg C (375 deg F). Lightly grease with butter a 23 cm (9 in) springform pan and line base with baking parchment. Sift the flour with the baking powder.

Beat the butter and sugar until creamy, light and fluffy. Add the eggs gradually, beating all the time. Fold in the sifted flour. Then add the milk and the co-coconut. Pour the mixture into the prepared pan and bake for 20 minutes or until the cake has shrunk slightly away from the sides of the pan. Turn the cake out onto a wire rack to cool. When cool, pour glacé icing over the top of the cake and sprinkle with coconut.

25

CONFECTIONERS' CUSTARD

250 ml (8 fl oz) cream (single)
250 ml (8 fl oz) milk
150 g (5 oz) caster (superfine) sugar
75 ml (3 fl oz) milk, extra
100 ml (4 fl oz) cream (single), extra
75 g (3 oz) cornflour (corn starch)
3 eggs, lightly beaten
4 level teaspoons gelatine
35 ml (1 ½ fl oz) water

COMBINE the cream, milk and sugar in a saucepan and bring to the boil. Remove from the heat. Mix together the extra milk, extra cream, cornflour and eggs. Pour the hot mixture over the cold mixture, stirring all the time. Cook over a medium heat until the custard boils and thickens, stirring all the time.

Sprinkle the gelatine over the water in a small bowl and soak for 5 to 10 minutes until softened. Stand in a pan of hot water until the gelatine has fully dissolved. Stir the water and gelatine into the hot custard. Use as required. Makes 900 ml (32 fl oz) of custard.

DANISH APPLE CAKE

250 g (9 oz) plain (all-purpose) flour
2 teaspoons cream of tartar
1 teaspoon bicarbonate of soda (baking soda)
100 g (4 oz) butter
250 g (9 oz) sugar
2 eggs, well beaten
250 ml (8 fl oz) milk
2 green cooking apples, peeled, cored and thinly sliced
1 teaspoon powdered cinnamon

PREHEAT oven to 200 deg C (400 deg F). Lightly grease with butter a 23 cm (9 in) springform pan or cake pan and line with baking parchment. Sift the flour with the cream of tartar and bicarbonate of soda.

Rub the butter into the flour. Stir in the sugar. Add the eggs beating very well after they are added. Gently stir in the milk and mix thoroughly. Pour the mixture into the prepared pan. Spread over the mixture a layer of thinly sliced apples and sprinkle with the cinnamon. Bake for 25 minutes or until the

cake has shrunk slightly away from the side of the pan. Turn out onto a wire rack to cool.

DARK CAKE

350 g (12 oz) plain (all-purpose) flour
2 teaspoons baking powder
2 teaspoons mixed spice
1 teaspoon cinnamon
250 g (9 oz) butter
250 g (9 oz) sugar
4 eggs
250 ml (8 fl oz) milk
250 g (9 oz) treacle (molasses)
160 g (5 ½ oz) raisins
160 g (5 ½ oz) currants

PREHEAT oven to 180 deg C (350 deg F). Generously grease a 23 cm (9 in) springform pan or cake pan with butter and line with baking parchment. Sift the flour with the baking powder, mixed spice and cinnamon.

Beat the butter and sugar until creamy, light and fluffy. Add the eggs one at a time, beating very well after each one is added. Mix in by hand the sifted flour and the milk. Stir in the treacle (molasses), raisins and currants. Pour the mixture into the prepared pan and bake for two hours or until the cake has shrunk slightly away from the sides of the pan.

When stoning dates,
rub butter on the knife and your fingers,
and the dates will not stick.

29

DATE CAKE

250 ml (8 fl oz) water
1 teaspoon bicarbonate of soda (baking soda)
160 g (5 ½ oz) dates
250 g (9 oz) plain (all-purpose) flour
2 teaspoons baking powder
225 g (8 oz) butter
250 g (9 oz) sugar
2 eggs, well beaten
150 g (5 oz) walnuts, chopped

DISSOLVE bicarbonate of soda in water and pour over dates and leave to soak overnight.

Preheat oven to 180 deg C (350 deg F). Lightly grease with butter a 28 cm x 18 cm (11 in x 7 in) cake pan and line the base with baking parchment. Sift the flour with the baking powder.

Beat the butter and sugar until creamy, light and fluffy. Add the eggs one at a time, beating very well after each one is added. Mix in the walnuts and the dates with their liquid then stir in by hand the sifted flour. Pour the mixture into the prepared pan and bake for 1 hour or until the cake has shrunk slightly away from the sides of the pan. Turn the cake out onto a wire rack to cool.

31

ECONOMICAL GOLDEN FRUIT CAKE

250 g (9 oz) plain (all-purpose) flour
2 level teaspoons baking powder
125 g (4 ½ oz) sugar
125 g (4 ½ oz) sultanas (golden raisins)
½ teaspoon salt
1 teaspoon mixed spice
2 tablespoons golden (light corn) syrup
250 ml (8 fl oz) warm milk
finely grated rind of 1 orange
juice of 1 orange

PREHEAT oven to 180 deg C (350 deg F). Generously grease a 20 cm x 10 cm x 5 cm (8 in x 4 in x 2 in) bar pan with butter and line with baking parchment. Sift the flour with the baking powder.

Mix together sifted flour, sugar, sultanas, salt and mixed spice. Dissolve golden syrup in warm milk. Add orange rind and juice to milk mixture then stir into the dry ingredients. Combine well. Pour the mixture into the prepared pan and bake for 40 minutes or until the cake has shrunk slightly away from the sides of the pan.

GALLIPOLI TEA CAKE

375 g (13 oz) plain (all-purpose) flour
1 teaspoon bicarbonate of soda (baking soda)
2 teaspoons cream of tartar
1 small teaspoon salt
1 tablespoon butter
250 g (9 oz) sugar
2 eggs
375 ml (13 fl oz) milk

Topping
75 g (3 oz) plain (all-purpose) flour, sifted
75 g (3 oz) sugar
50 g (2 oz) butter
1 teaspoon of ground cinnamon

PREHEAT oven to 180 deg C (350 deg F). Lightly grease with butter a 23 cm (9 in) springform pan or cake pan and line base with baking parchment. Sift the flour with the bicarbonate of soda, cream of tartar and salt.

Beat the butter and sugar until creamy, light and fluffy. Add the eggs one at a time, beating very well after each one is added. Gently fold in by hand the sifted flour alternately with a little milk. Pour the mixture into the prepared pan. To make the topping rub the butter into the flour, sugar and cinnamon and sprinkle over the top of the cake mixture. Bake for 30 to 40 minutes.

Gingerbread

---

375 g (13 oz) plain (all-purpose) flour
175 g (6 oz) butter
1 tablespoon ground ginger
2 teaspoons cinnamon
½ teaspoon allspice
175 g (6 oz) brown sugar
350 g (12 oz) golden (light corn) syrup
1 egg, beaten
250 ml (8 fl oz) warm milk with 1 teaspoon bicarbonate of soda
(baking soda) dissolved in it

PREHEAT oven to 180 deg C (350 deg F). Grease a large loaf pan lightly with butter and line with baking parchment. Sift the flour.

Beat the butter with the ginger, cinnamon and allspice. Gradually add the sugar, beating until creamy and smooth. Mix in the golden syrup. Add the beaten egg gradually to the creamed mixture, beating all the time. Gently fold in by hand the sifted flour alternately with the milk and mix thoroughly.

THEIR POPULARITY WILL ASTONISH YOU

Crisp, dainty biscuits, designed to enhance the delicate flavours of savoury items. They look nice, they taste nice and please everyone. They add a new grace and tempting quality to bridge and afternoon teas. Ask your grocer for "Savoury Dainties," "Lawn Tennis Soda," "Small Cheese" and "Thin Captain."

ARNOTT'S

FAMOUS

BISCUITS FOR SAVOURIES

Always ask your grocer for Arnott's. They are better than ever.

Pour the mixture into the prepared pan and bake for 1 hour and 20 minutes or until the cake has shrunk slightly away from the sides of the pan and a skewer inserted in the centre comes out clean. Turn out onto a wire rack to cool.

GINGER SPONGE

185 g (6 ½ oz) plain (all-purpose) flour
2 level teaspoons baking powder
1 ½ teaspoons mixed spice
1 teaspoon ground ginger
75 g (3 oz) butter
225 g (8 oz) sugar
2 eggs, beaten
175 g (6 oz) golden (light corn) syrup
150 ml (5 fl oz) milk
preserved ginger, chopped

PREHEAT oven to 180 deg C (350 deg F). Grease two 18 cm (7 in) springform pans (or sandwich pans) lightly with butter and line bases with baking parchment. Sift the flour with the baking powder, mixed spice and ground ginger.

Beat the butter and sugar until creamy, light and fluffy. Add the beaten eggs gradually, beating all the time. Mix together the golden syrup and milk and stir into the mixture. Fold in the sifted flour. Pour the mixture into the prepared pans and bake for 20 minutes or until the cakes have shrunk slightly away from the sides of the pan. Turn the cakes out onto a wire rack to cool. When cool, join the cakes together with whipped cream and preserved ginger. Pour coffee flavoured glacé icing over the top of the cake.

GLACE ICING

225 g (8 oz) icing sugar
2 tablespoons water

S IFT icing sugar so that it is free of lumps. Put it into a bowl and add water until it is the consistency of thick treacle (molasses). Stand the bowl in a saucepan of hot water, stirring until it becomes thin enough to pour easily. Pour over cake and spread evenly with a knife. A teaspoon of butter may be added, or fruit juices can be used instead of water.

Flavourings for 225 g (8 oz) Glacé Icing
Chocolate/cocoa powder — 1 level tablespoon
Coffee — 2 tablespoons coffee or 1 teaspoon coffee essence
Lemon — Strained juice of 1 lemon and water to make up 2 tablespoons
Orange — 2 tablespoons orange juice.
Essence or extract — Add a few drops to the water.

JELLY CAKE

225 g (8 oz) flour
1 1/2 teaspoons baking powder
115 g (4 ¼ oz) butter
85 g (3 ½ oz) sugar
3 eggs
4 tablespoons milk
2 tablespoons red jelly crystals
red jelly crystals, extra

PREHEAT oven to 180 deg C (350 deg F). Lightly grease with butter a 20 cm (8 in) springform pan or cake pan and line base with baking parchment. Sift the flour with the baking powder.

Beat the butter and sugar until creamy, light and fluffy. Add the eggs one at a time, beating very well after each one is added. Gently fold in by hand the sifted flour alternately with the milk.

Mix in the jelly crystals and pour the mixture into the prepared pan. Bake for 30 minutes or until the top of the cake springs back when lightly touched and the cake has shrunk slightly away from the sides of the pan. Cool for 5 minutes before turning out onto a wire rack to cool. Cut the cake in half and fill with cream. Cover the cake with glacé icing and sprinkle with jelly crystals.

LAMINGTONS

125 g (4 ½ oz) plain (all-purpose) flour
1/2 teaspoon baking powder
125 g (4 ½ oz) butter
185 g (6 ½ oz) sugar
4 eggs

Icing
500g (1 lb 1 oz) icing sugar
50 g (2 oz) plain chocolate
2 ½ tablespoons water
vanilla

P REHEAT oven to 180 deg C (350 deg F). Lightly grease with butter a 20 cm x 20 cm (8 in x 8 in) square cake pan and line with baking parchment. Sift flour with the baking powder.

Beat the butter and sugar until creamy, light and fluffy. Add the eggs one at a time, beating very well after each one is added. Gently fold into the creamed mixture the sifted flour. Pour the mixture into the prepared pan. Bake until golden brown and the sides are shrinking away from the pan. Cool. When cold cut into square blocks. Slice each block into three slices and fill with raspberry jam.

Sift the icing sugar and grate the chocolate. Put the sugar and chocolate in a saucepan with the water. Heat, stirring all the time but do not allow to boil. When it is quite liquid add the vanilla. Remove from heat.

To coat the blocks with chocolate icing secure them with a fork or skewer then dip them into the icing, coating them on all sides. Drain off excess icing and immediately roll the blocks in a large dish of desiccated coconut. Allow to dry before storing.

Add eggs gradually to beaten butter and sugar; if added too quickly the mixture will curdle and the cake will be coarse. If eggs start to curdle, immediately add a little flour.

MADEIRA CAKE

---

275 g (10 oz) plain (all-purpose) flour
1 teaspoon baking powder
½ teaspoon salt
225 g (8 oz) butter
225 g (8 oz) caster (superfine) sugar
finely grated rind of 1 lemon and 1 orange
½ teaspoon ground cinnamon
5 eggs
1 tablespoon milk

P REHEAT oven to 160 deg C (325 deg F). Lightly grease with butter a 20 cm (8 in) springform pan or cake pan and line with baking parchment. Sift the flour with the baking powder and salt.

Beat the butter and sugar until creamy, light and fluffy. Mix in the grated orange and lemon rind with the cinnamon. Add the eggs one at a time, beating very well after each one is added. Gently fold in by hand the sifted flour alternately with the milk. Pour the mixture into the prepared pan. Bake for 1 ½ hours or until a skewer placed in the centre comes out clean.

MARBLE CAKE

275 g (10 oz) plain (all-purpose) flour
2 teaspoons baking powder
160 g (5 ½ oz) butter
215 g (7 ½ oz) caster (superfine) sugar
3 eggs
250 ml (8 fl oz) milk
red food colouring
35g (1 ½ oz) cocoa powder

P REHEAT oven to 180 deg C (350 deg F). Grease a loaf pan lightly with butter and line base with baking parchment. Sift together flour and baking powder.

Beat the butter and sugar until creamy, light and fluffy. Add the eggs one at a time, beating very well after each one is added. Gently fold in by hand the flour alternately with the milk. Divide mixture into three. Mix in a few drops of red food colouring to one, mix the cocoa powder into the second and leave the last one plain. Place large spoonfuls of each mixture alternately in the prepared pan. Bake for 35 to 40 minutes until the cake has shrunk slightly away from the sides of the pan. Turn out onto a wire rack. When cold decorate with glacé icing.

MINCE TARTS

Fruit Mince
250 g (9 oz) sultanas (golden raisins)
400 g (14 oz) raisins, chopped
125 g (4 ½ oz) currants
125 g (4 ½ oz) mixed peel
250 g (9 oz) sugar
2 large cooking apples, peeled, cored and grated
1 lemon, grated rind and juice
1 orange, grated rind and juice
1 level teaspoon mixed spice
pinch of salt
4 tablespoons brandy
185 g (6 ½ oz) suet, finely grated

Pastry
375 g (14 oz) plain (all-purpose) flour
1 teaspoon baking powder
pinch of salt
185 g (6 ½ oz) butter
175 g (6 ½ oz) icing sugar
2 egg yolks
1 tablespoon water
few drops vanilla

T O MAKE the fruit mince: combine the sultanas, raisins, currants, mixed peel, sugar, grated apples, lemon rind and juice, orange rind and juice, mixed spice, salt and brandy. Mix well. Add the finely grated suet. Stand at least overnight in a covered container. Store the fruit mince in a covered container in the refrigerator for up to several weeks but allow to return to room temperature before using.

Preheat oven to 180 deg C (350 deg F). Grease a patty pan (cup cake pan) lightly with butter.

To make the pastry: sift the flour with the baking powder and salt into a bowl. Rub in the butter until it resembles breadcrumbs. Stir in the sifted icing sugar and make a well in the centre. Add egg yolks, water and vanilla. Mix to a soft dough. Knead lightly until smooth, wrap and chill at least one hour.

Roll pastry out thinly and cut into rounds. Place the rounds in the prepared pan and fill them with fruit mince. Brush the edges of the rounds with cold water then cover with another round of pastry. Decorate the edges with a fork and brush with beaten egg or milk. Bake for about 15 minutes. Cool in the pans for 5 minutes before turning out onto wire racks to cool.

NAPOLEONS

225 g (8 oz) puff or flaky pastry
jam
1 sponge cake made in a
Swiss (jelly) roll tin (see Swiss roll recipe)

P REHEAT oven to 200 deg C (400 deg F). Grease a baking tray (sheet) lightly with butter.

Roll the pastry till it is twice the size of the Swiss roll tray. Cut off uneven edges. Cut pastry in half across the length, and score one piece of pastry with the shapes wanted for the Napoleons. Bake pastry for 10 minutes or until nicely browned. Spread the unscored pastry with jam, and place sponge on top; spread

Make your home
TRULY MODERN

sponge with jam, and place the other pastry on top. Trim outside edges so that they are even. Cover with glacé icing and sprinkle with chopped almonds. Cut into marked shapes.

If liked, sponge cake can be split through and filled with cream before putting together with pastry.

If oranges are bought a week before using, and placed in a warm room, they will be sweeter, juicy, and easy to peel.

ORANGE CAKE

250 g (9 oz) (all-purpose) flour
2 teaspoons baking powder
pinch of salt
250 g (9 oz) butter
rind of 1 large orange
250 g (9 oz) caster (superfine) sugar
4 eggs
juice of 1 large orange

PREHEAT oven to 180 deg C (350 deg F). Grease a large loaf pan lightly with butter and line with baking parchment. Sift the flour with the baking powder and salt.

Beat the butter and sugar until creamy, light and fluffy. Mix in the grated orange rind. Add the eggs one at a time, beating very well after each one is added. Gently fold into the creamed mixture the flour alternately with the orange juice. Pour the mixture into the prepared pan. Bake for 45 minutes or until a skewer placed in the centre comes out clean. Decorate with glacé icing flavoured with 1 tablespoon of grated orange rind and 1 tablespoon of orange juice.

PASSIONFRUIT CAKE

275 g (10 oz) plain (all-purpose) flour
1 teaspoon baking powder
225 g (8 oz) butter
225 g (8 oz) sugar
5 eggs
6 passionfruit

P REHEAT oven to 180 deg C (350 deg F). Grease two 18 cm (7 in) springform pans (or sandwich pans) lightly with butter and line bases with baking parchment. Sift the flour with the baking powder.

Beat the butter and sugar until creamy, light and fluffy. Add the eggs one at a time, beating very well after each one is added. Mix in by hand the sifted flour. Beat well and fold in the passionfruit. Pour the mixture into the prepared pans and bake for 15 to 20 minutes or until the cakes have shrunk slightly away from the sides of the pan. Turn the cakes out onto a wire rack to cool. When cool, slice the cakes in half and join layers together with cream or passionfruit glacé icing. Decorate the top of the cake with passionfruit glacé icing.

QUEEN CAKES

100 g (4 oz) plain (all-purpose) flour
½ teaspoonful baking powder
100 g (4 oz) butter
100 g (4 oz) sugar
2 eggs
milk, if necessary
50 g (2 oz) sultanas (golden raisins)

PREHEAT oven to 200 deg C (400 deg F). Grease a patty pans (cup cake pans) or paper cases lightly with butter. Sift the flour and the baking powder.

Beat the butter and sugar until creamy, light and fluffy. Add the eggs one at a time, beating very well after each one is added.

Gently fold in by hand the sifted flour together with a little milk if necessary, to give a soft dropping consistency. Add the fruit, and place spoonfuls of the mixture in the pans or papers. Bake for 15 to 20 minutes, until firm to the touch and golden brown colour.

RICH CHOCOLATE CAKE

225g (8 oz) plain (all-purpose) flour
35g (1 ½ oz) cocoa powder
1 ½ teaspoonfuls baking powder
pinch of salt
100 g (4 oz) butter
100 g (4 oz) caster (superfine) sugar
2 eggs
vanilla
150 ml (5 fl oz) milk, approximately

P REHEAT oven to 190 deg C (375 deg F). Lightly grease with butter an 18 cm (7 in) springform pan or cake pan. Sift the flour and the baking powder, cocoa powder and salt.

Beat the butter and sugar until creamy, light and fluffy. Add the eggs one at a time, beating very well after each one is added. Mix in a few drops of vanilla. Gently fold in by hand the sifted flour together with enough milk to give a soft dropping consistency. Pour into the prepared pan and bake for 1 to 1 ½ hours or until the cake has shrunk slightly away from the sides of the pan and a skewer inserted in the middle comes out clean.

When the cake is cool, it may either be dredged with icing sugar or coated with glacé icing.

SEED CAKE

250 g (9 oz) plain (all-purpose)
flour
1 teaspoon baking powder
4 tablespoons hot water
250 g (9 oz) sugar
225 g (8 oz) butter
2 eggs
pinch of salt
1 dessertspoon caraway seeds

PREHEAT oven to 180 deg C (350 deg F). Grease a 23 cm (9 in) springform pan lightly with butter and line with baking parchment. Sift half the flour. Sift the remaining half of the flour with the baking powder.

Place the hot water in a bowl

49

then add the sugar so that it begins to melt. Beat the butter into this until it is creamy, light and fluffy. Add the eggs one at a time, beating very well after each one is added. Fold in the flour that has no baking powder with the salt and beat for five minutes. Add the caraway seeds and then the flour sifted with the baking powder and beat for another five minutes. Pour the mixture into the prepared pan. Bake for 1 hour or until the cake has shrunk slightly away from the sides of the pan.

SULTANA CAKE

1 teaspoon bicarbonate of soda (baking soda)
250 ml (8 fl oz) cold water
350 g (12 oz) sultanas (golden raisins)
275 g (10 oz) plain (all-purpose) flour
225 g (8 oz) butter
250 g (9 oz) sugar
2 eggs

DISSOLVE bicarbonate of soda in water, then pour over sultanas and leave to soak overnight.
Preheat oven to 180 deg C (350 deg F). Grease a 23 cm (9 in) springform pan or cake pan well with butter and line the base with baking parchment. Sift the flour.

Beat the butter and sugar until creamy, light and fluffy. Add the eggs one at a time, beating very well after each one is added. Stir in the sultanas and their liquid then mix in by hand the sifted flour. Thoroughly combine. Pour the mixture into the prepared pan and bake for 2 ½ hours or until the cake has shrunk slightly away from the sides of the pan. Turn the cake out onto a wire rack to cool.

Everything turns out perfectly

since I've had my

Sunbeam MIXMASTER

"After looking at all sorts of mixers and mixing gadgets I decided on a Sunbeam Mixmaster—a wonderful decision I'll never regret. My Mixmaster does *everything* better . . . It mixes big, 6-lb. mixtures in one 'go,' and some cakes, like this one, *in only 3 minutes* . . . Puddings, too, and things like scones, omelettes, cookies and meringues all turn out perfectly . . . What's more, my Sunbeam Mixmaster mashes, beats, folds, juices, whips, creams, stirs and blends—all quickly, all easily. Believe me, there's nothing like a Sunbeam Mixmaster."

ONLY SUNBEAM MIXMASTER HAS ALL THESE FEATURES . . . IT'S A REAL FOOD MIXER

Streamlined Beauty

Gleaming black and white finish— the perfect colour-toning

SUNBEAM BOWL-SPEED CONTROL.
A special nylon button fitted to one of the Mixmaster beaters contacts the inside surface of the bowl and turns the bowl automatically on a revolving disc, thus keeping bowl-speed and beater-speed uniform.

SUNBEAM MIX-FINDER DIAL.
Selects scientifically correct beating speeds for *all* food-mixing tasks. Hundreds of different speeds may be "tuned in" to meet individual requirements.

SUNBEAM BEATER EJECTOR.
Automatically ejects the glistening Sunbeam "full mix" beaters by simply flicking the handle. No unscrewing—no messy fingers.

SUNBEAM JUICE EXTRACTOR.
Gets all the juice automatically, faster, cleaner.

SUNBEAM PORTABILITY.
Take the beaters to a saucepan on the stove, simply, easily, safely—nothing to go wrong.

SUNBEAM BEATER ADJUSTMENT LEVER.
Adjusts correct beater position for both bowls—automatically.

FULL-POWER MOTOR.
The powerful governor-controlled Sunbeam motor, with power to spare, gives smooth running and even mixing on every speed . . . handling up to 6 lbs. of mixture at once.

Made and guaranteed by Sunbeam CORPORATION LTD., Sydney. Sold by authorised electrical dealers and leading department stores throughout Australia.

Swiss roll pan and lining paper must be well greased
if cake is to come out easily.

SWISS ROLL
(OR JELLY ROLL)

75 g (3 oz) plain (all-purpose) flour
1 teaspoon baking powder
pinch of salt
3 eggs
125 g (4 ½ oz) caster (superfine) sugar
1 tablespoon hot water
4 tablespoons hot jam
caster (superfine) sugar, extra

PREHEAT oven to 200 deg C (400 deg F). Grease a Swiss (jelly) roll pan lightly with butter and line with greased baking parchment. Mix the flour, baking powder and salt and sift twice.

Using an electric mixer beat the eggs and sugar until they become very thick and creamy. Gently fold in by hand the sifted flour and the hot water. Pour the mixture into the prepared pan and bake for 10 to 15 minutes or until the top of the cake springs back when lightly touched and the cake has shrunk slightly away from the sides of the pan.

Sprinkle a teatowel with plenty of caster sugar. Turn the sponge out, on to the teatowel, immediately it is removed from the oven. Peel off the baking parchment. Trim the crisp edges off with a sharp knife. Roll up the sponge in the towel and leave it to cool.

In a saucepan gently warm the jam. Unroll the sponge

52

COOKERY

carefully. Spread the jam over the sponge leaving about 2.5 cm (1 in) around the edges.

Roll the sponge into a neat firm roll using the teatowel to help. With the join underneath sprinkle the roll with extra caster sugar.

Cakes should always be turned on to a wire rack to cool.

TEA CAKE

200 g (7 oz) plain (all-purpose) flour
2 level teaspoons baking powder
125 g (4 ½ oz) sugar
1 egg
185 ml (6 ½ fl oz) milk
150 g (5 oz) sultanas (golden raisins)
1 teaspoon butter
1 dessertspoon caster sugar
½ teaspoon cinnamon

PREHEAT oven to 180 deg C (350 deg F). Grease two 18 cm (7 in) springform pans (or sandwich pans) lightly with butter and line bases with baking parchment. Sift the flour with the baking powder.

Beat the sugar and egg until creamy. Add the milk and gradually fold in the sifted flour. Mix in the sultanas and pour the mixture into the prepared pans. Bake for 25 minutes or until the cakes have shrunk slightly away from the sides of the pans. Turn the cakes out onto a wire rack to cool. While they are still warm, rub the butter over the top and sprinkle generously with sugar and cinnamon.

Eggs come in several different sizes.
Standard cooking eggs are 55 g (about 2 ½ oz). It is best
to cook with eggs at room temperature.

UPSIDEDOWN APRICOT CAKE

150 g (5 oz) plain (all-purpose) flour
2 level teaspoons baking powder
pinch of salt
2 tablespoons butter, melted
50 g (2 oz) brown sugar
4 apricots, halved, must be firm, not soft and over-ripe
1 egg
75 ml (3 fl oz) melted butter
150 ml (5 fl oz) milk
85 g (3 ½ oz) raw sugar

PREHEAT oven to 180 deg C (350 deg F). Sift the flour with the baking powder and salt. Pour the melted butter into the base of an 18 cm (7 in) springform pan or cake pan. Evenly

spread the brown sugar across the base. Place the eight apricot halves cut side down on top of the brown sugar.

Separately beat the egg and mix in the 75 ml (3 fl oz) of melted butter. Stir in the milk. Combine the sifted flour with the raw sugar. Fold these dry ingredients into the egg mixture and beat very vigorously for

1 minute. Pour the mixture carefully over the apricots in the prepared pan and smooth the surface. Bake for 45 minutes. Allow to cool slightly then turn out carefully onto a wire rack to cool.

Gelatine powder needs to be completely dissolved before using it. Gelatine becomes leathery if it is kept a long time so it is best used immediately.

VANILLA SLICES

225 g (8 oz) puff or flaky pastry
custard (see confectioners' custard recipe)
1 large tablespoon cornflour (corn starch)
600 ml (20 fl oz) milk
sugar
vanilla

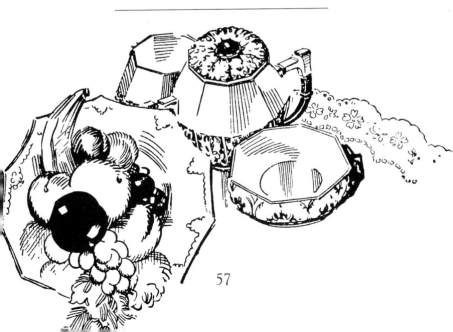

57

Preheat oven to 200 deg C (400 deg F). Grease a baking tray (sheet) lightly with butter.

Roll pastry into a thin sheet. Place on oven tray and make little cuts all over pastry to prevent rising. Cut into two even pieces and cook until lightly golden brown. Make custard, and when both the pastry and the custard are cool, cover one half of the pastry with the custard, and place the other half of the pastry on top of custard. Spread with glacé icing and cut into squares.

VICTORIA SPONGE

250 g (9 oz) plain (all-purpose) flour
2 teaspoons baking powder
pinch of salt
250 g (9 oz) butter
225 g (8 oz) caster (superfine) sugar
vanilla
4 eggs

P REHEAT oven to 190 deg C (375 deg F). Grease two 18 cm (7 in) springform pans (or sandwich pans) lightly with butter and line with baking parchment. Sift the flour with the baking powder and salt.

Beat the butter and sugar until creamy, light and fluffy. Mix in the vanilla. Add the eggs one at a time, beating very well after each one is added. Gently fold in by hand the sifted flour. Pour the mixture into the prepared pans and bake for 40 to 45 minutes or until the top of the cake springs back when lightly touched and the cakes have shrunk slightly away from the sides of the trays. Cool in the pans for 5 minutes before turning out onto wire racks to cool. Sandwich together with jam and whipped cream and dust the top with icing sugar.

WALNUT LOAF

200 g (7 oz) (all-purpose) flour
2 teaspoons baking powder
pinch of salt
50 g (2 oz) butter
125 g (4 ½ oz) sugar
1 egg, beaten
125 ml (4 ½ fl oz) milk
75 g (3 oz) walnuts, roughly chopped

PREHEAT oven to 180 deg C (350 deg F). Grease a cylindrical nut loaf pan or rectangular loaf pan generously with butter and line with baking parchment. Sift the flour with the baking powder and salt.

Beat the butter and sugar until creamy, light and fluffy. Add the egg, beating very well. Combine the sifted flour and the nuts. Gently fold into the creamed mixture the flour alternately with the milk. Mix in the walnuts. Spoon the mixture into the prepared pan. Bake for 1 hour. Turn out onto a cake rack to cool. This is best made the day before it is to be eaten.

To beat egg whites successfully you
should always use a metal or a glass bowl.
Egg whites are best used at room temperature
and must not have any of the yolk in them.
Never overbeat egg whites.

WEDDING CAKE

275 g (10 oz) plain (all-purpose) flour
¼ level teaspoon baking powder
¼ level teaspoon mixed spice
¼ level teaspoon nutmeg
good pinch of salt
225 g (8 oz) butter
100 g (4 oz) light brown sugar
100 g (4 oz) white sugar
4 eggs
350 g (12 oz) raisins
350 g (12 oz) sultanas (golden raisins)
225 g (8 oz) currants
100 g (4 oz) mixed peel
100 g (4 oz) glacé cherries
100 g (4 oz) blanched and chopped almonds
4 tablespoons brandy, sherry or whisky

THE DAY before the cake is to be made, chop the fruit into similar sized pieces. Sprinkle with half the brandy, sherry or whisky. Cover and set aside.

Preheat oven to 180 deg C (350 deg F). Generously grease a 20 cm (8 in) springform pan or cake pan with butter and line with two layers of brown paper and two layers of baking parchment. Sift the flour with the baking powder, spices and salt.

Beat the butter and sugars until creamy, light and fluffy. Add the eggs one at a time, beating very well after each one is added. Mix in half the fruit and the remaining brandy, sherry or whisky. Fold in half the sifted flour. Add the remaining fruit to the

61

mixture and fold in the remaining flour. Mix well. Spoon the mixture carefully into the prepared pan and smooth the surface. Bake for 3 to 3 ½ hours.

The cake should be made six to eight weeks before the wedding to allow it time to mature.

One teaspoon each of finely grated lemon and orange rind could also be added when creaming the butter and sugar, if liked.

Lining the tins is very important. The papers must be smoothed carefully into the corners so that the cakes will have a smooth surface for icing

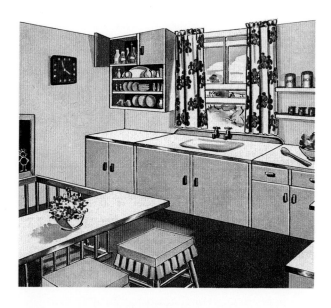

63

ACKNOWLEDGEMENTS

With thanks to all the good friends who delved into their recipe collections, particularly Katrina Pizzini and her mother.

Also many thanks to the following companies for their help Arnott's Biscuits Limited, Big Sister Foods Limited, Cadbury Schweppes Pty. Ltd., Hoover (Aust) Pty. Ltd., Letona Foods, Sanitarium Health Food Co., Taubmans Industries Pty. Ltd., Sunbeam Victa Corporation and Unifoods Pty. Ltd.